A SMIDGEN OF IRISH LUCK

A Woman's Musings on her Travels to Ireland

By Kay Thomas

Kay Thomas

Author of …**AND ONE MORE THING I Brake for Squirrels and Other Thoughts I Have No Doubt About**

ISBN-13: 978-1496100047

Author information at www.kathomaswriter.com
Thomas's blog www.overaroundhills.blogspot.com

DEDICATION

For a wee redheaded Irish girl listening to a singer in a thatched roof pub.

To all my readers and friends who are curious as to what I do on my days off.

To reluctant solo travelers — Go.

smidgen- *a small portion of something; English word of Scottish Gaelic origin.*

INTRODUCTION

A solitary yellow wildflower on steep stone stairs captures my deepest sentiment. I do not realize that a tiny flora is forcing me to contemplate my larger purpose in life.

Every hillside has its flock of sheep, and fellow tourists complain that it is monotonous. Catching a little snooze and counting sheep while the wheels of the bus go round and round, is not for me. In its place I create unique stories in my mind of hardship and starvation on the scattered rocks in the rugged scenery complete with a cast of imaginary characters.

I see things differently than other travelers. When I am on my own it becomes even more apparent. All my senses combined are on high alert, and experiences get absorbed until I feel my head bursting with stimulation like pinpricks all over my scalp. Interestingly, I dare say that certain of these nuggets resurface, but I suspect that the majority lay hidden within me peacefully forever.

A practiced attentiveness causes me to stay in the moment until I see the extraordinary out of the ordinary. Living in a rural environment for years is helpful in harmonious compatibility with nature. My eyes are roving constantly, and the slightest movement or shadow signals me to sit up and take notice.

These essays are rightfully titled, "A Smidgen of Irish Luck," for it is the bits and pieces of me leftover from a trip that I portion out to you one at a time.

If you follow my newspaper column, AND ONE MORE THING..., in the *Livingston County News*, Geneseo, NY, then you will no doubt be surprised at an unfamiliar voice coming through in these essays. I blame it on the Irish. And I am serious about it, too. Ireland has a way of seeping into my soul, you know, and I get sucked right into the culture like nowhere else I have ever traveled in the world. That's someone with no Irish blood talking, too.

Besides, I am a lover of Irish literature, and thanks to diligent college professors that I see the value of the language; authors and poets are my friends. I'll tackle Yeats and Heaney, along with William James, for another read through any time I have the urge to ruffle my state of being. Certain passages are best read aloud to follow the natural rhyme and cadence of the Irish author like listening to a story in the town pub. I have this journey to discover that fact.

When I leave home I fully intend to keep a daily journal on my laptop. I have no clue what I will be writing when I return. It usually happens, though, that little tidbits stick in my head, and re-reading notes will prompt me to start a piece or two at the oddest hour of the night.

It doesn't work this time. My computer sputters and crashes the first couple days while I am in Belfast.

Somehow, I never can go back to writing on paper. I let it all go, take my chances and never think twice about it.

One thing I "hear" loud and clear is a beautiful Irish lilt so lovely to the ears. Waiting in the airport lounge before leaving for Belfast, I overhear a family chatting together, and I take it all in trying to get into the flavor of what will come.

Surprisingly, about a month after I arrive home, I find I need to be writing, and day and night thoughts come together in dreams and early morning vignettes. The weather is optimal, and here I am sitting inside in my windowless office letting words flow. That's me, though. The time is right.

Thanks to the encouragement of my readers, writing friends and family, I decide to publish this volume. Truthfully, without them, it might not see light of day.

You will see a different side of me. Better yet, you might be prompted to try an Irish adventure, if you haven't already gone to The Emerald Isle.

Traveling Starts at Home

The journey not the arrival matters. – T. S. Eliot

My journey begins on the last day of February 2013. The exact date doesn't really matter. I write it down to show how in my estimation the trip to Ireland is way longer than the actual three weeks touring both Northern Ireland and the Republic of Ireland.

The decision to travel on my own is settled, and I have three months to immerse myself in everything Irish — literature, poetry and travelogues in order to get the most out of my vacation. Even the weather is a concern, and I face the fact that it must not get in the way of sightseeing.

Not knowing my fellow travelers a head of time brings me to the realization that I *am* a friendly person, and I will do just fine meeting others sharing a love for adventure.

Besides, I wonder what it is like to see things through all my senses with a plan to write upon my return without talking it out with any other living soul on the spot.

I list things (a woman concern) to purchase — new lightweight suitcase and waterproof gear, after I evaluate what I already have in my closet that might suffice from past trips.

I find it amazing how much I already know from world travel — like changing money efficiently and how to find my way back to a hotel — that resurfaces at odd moments when I am not even thinking in that direction.

A second listing of what I need to know, to get comfortable with all the technology — laptop, iPhone, camera and assorted plugs, cords and extensions. Formerly, I am lazy (sigh) and turn that over to my husband. Now I have to step-up and figure things out.

I love all the analyzing that I have to do throughout the early spring. I know that the better I prepare, the more that I will get out of the trip.

On top of it all, there is a constant nagging sensation about going it alone. I use a mantra that will be invaluable through out. Whenever I get panicky about a trip on which I have paid out hundreds of dollars, I say it over to myself.

"You can do it."

As you read the essays in this collection, you decide for yourself how well I accomplished my mission.

My journey ends on June 24, 2013 when I arrive home safely with memories that will linger forever, assorted souvenirs and a joyful heart.

"I did it."

Between my finger and my thumb
The squat pen rests.
I'll dig with it.
"Digging"
Seamus Heaney
(1939-2013)

Marking Time in 26D

Hello. My name is 26D.

At least that's who the flimsy rectangular paper states I am.

For the next six hours and thirty-five minutes I will be generically classified as an older female. Caucasian. No distinguishing features.

There is no need to refer to me by birth name, surname, or any other information required on my driver's license or passport. My vital statistics are tucked away along with my Twitter account and Facebook page.

I am one of 295 passengers with a final destination of Belfast, Ireland. From years and years of flying, I know that this necessary travel ordeal must be tolerated like the dark clothing and no jewelry rule I faithfully maintain so as not to announce to the world that I am alone. There is no way around it. I visualize the vacation waiting for me, and I accept jumping over the hurdles to achieve it.

Thus, the slow traipse commences to 26D clutching my boarding pass like a graduate in a college processional with her diploma seeking a new path.

My new identity: Two dozen plus two more. An even number. (Divide it by two, and it could be another story. I am not prone to superstition, though.)

It's my assigned fate—left-hand side, three-fourths to the rear past the wings. A bank of high seats in front of me, and the dense ocean below will obstruct my view most of the night.

Group 5 is the next to last group to board at Newark's Liberty International Airport on flight 077, an intriguing number designation for a hop over the pond to the British Commonwealth.

Like one of a multitude of human ants forward marching, I am a lemming creeping into the silver tube poised to navigate the friendly sky.

In six to eight minutes I will reach my row. My black, airplane-light carryon is put down to rest twelve times on the jet way during the interval. It is relatively quiet around me as the long line snakes its way.

A half look from busy flight attendants greets me at the open plane door. They have other things on their minds, and I will remain invisible. There are younger, more challenging men and women to chat up and flirt that they have already eyeballed. 26D will be served two meals and occasional water service. That's their obligation. No more. No less. Well, I am forgetting about my safety in case of____.

Inching down the aisle is tedious. For lack of anything better to occupy my mind, I examine my Taos black flat shoes guaranteed in the advertisement "to put a lift in my spirits, and my step," too. Not much gonna happen once I sit down and remove my shoes for the night.

One previous trip I brought an old pair of socks to walk the aisles for comfort before throwing them away at the end of the flight. Not so this trip. I'll do with putting my shoes back on so my feet don't touch the grooved floor of the lavatory smeared with tiny puddles of urine.

It's that hurry up and wait notion that makes no sense. I trod like a trooper, though, slinging my new waterproof black purse over my shoulder. It is bought particularly for its features—tons of hidden pockets, RAF pouch and thief-proof strap. I hope that purchase proves wise for anticipated rainy weather; although, I am a tiny bit concerned. Already it is heavy, and I don't have my camera weighing it down further. At the last minute I packed a small shoulder purse for dressy occasions, and later, I will come to thank myself.

Complete stop. Bottleneck.

Whack. I get smacked in the thigh from a suitcase like I expect sooner than later on any given flight leaving me slightly bruised days later in remembrance.

13A and B are a problem. Well, mostly B. Seat A is silent with thin lips pursed and arms folded. She is the one in charge by her nonverbal cues.

This infrequent, senior traveler is haphazardly slinging his luggage in the overhead wheels first with his arthritic swollen hands unsure if it will make the bin. He works at it. No fit. He re-adjusts the gray carryon. It fits.

13B moves into the row with his wife, also wearing her travel papers in a plastic sleeve around her neck. They are in their tan rollup sleeve travel shirts and matching wrinkle proof L.L. Bean sport pants ready for an adventure of a lifetime. They appear a little confused out of their daily comfort zone. Between the two of them, I have full faith that they will get through this grand trip. Their "big kids" at home will relax knowing mom and pops are still good to go for the time being. (Is my own wondering the same thoughts about me?)

It's a good pause to tug up my knee high black travel compression socks—a new style I selected from the catalog. I hope that they limit ankle swelling, a flight dilemma with medical consequences after landing.

Rows upon rows of humanity sit in seats facing forward waiting patiently for the takeoff. No one gives me more than a cursory glance.

19F.

A young mother in designer blue jeans tightly belted at the waist with a tucked in tee showing off her still cool figure with two school age kids in tow holds up the line while she buckles each one in and gives a last minute direction.

19F sits down in the row behind. Already she is searching for a move to get in the row with her children, and the art of negotiation begins. Musical chairs. Cross stretching and conversation. Playing computer games over and under the seats. Kids make friends easily.

Music is streaming from the sound system—the soothing elevator tracks lulling passengers into a quiet passivity. It is counting on me making fewer demands, staying in my seat, and watching dopy movies on my individual screen. From my past habits, I will leave my seat twice for stretching and bathroom trips. My monitor will stay on the travel route site, so I am able to watch our flight path.

22A.

A six-foot business traveler hurls his carry on up one-handed and sits down in his seat like he performs this routine every day of the year. He probably does. He hops up again when the coast is clear momentarily and takes off his suit jacket laying it with his luggage. He loosens his silk blue striped tie. He pulls out the Wall Street Journal, folds it in half, fourths and then efficiently organizes it to the article he wants to read.

26D.

I shuffle further and come to my aisle seat, the one I had requested.

26E and F.

The younger of the two men in the center seat greets me with a broad Cheshire cat grin on his chubby loompa face. It takes me off notice that he has put up the seat armrest, and he is spilling over into one-half of my seat, too.

Oh. I squeeze in what is left like a sausage—skinny can be helpful— thinking that this will add to the already arduous flight.

26E has a characteristic rising and falling of his voice when he speaks to 26F, an older look-a-like.

My intent is not to bond with 26E, and hope to make eye contact with a flight attendant to inquire if there might be an option for me.

More passengers pass by and the plane is filling up like the proverbial cattle car stuffed into every nook and cranny.

It doesn't look like I can move. I am stuck, and I face reality that 26E's arm rubbing mine will be what I rest on all night long to Belfast. It could be worse. He doesn't smell of body odor, and he isn't chanting with his prayer beads. I've had that happen on overnight flights. 26E seems pleasant enough, and the perfect person to pawn off the parts of my meal I don't touch—most of it.

I place my carryon overhead, and surprisingly, there is ample room for it. I slink down in the corner of my seat, fasten my seatbelt and wait.

My Kindle is loaded with bestselling books— Elizabeth Gilbert's *All Signature of Things* is high on my list— although I am uncertain it will be the right one to take me into its pages tonight. I remove my earphones from my purse—the airline ones are useless—and plug them in a search for a gentle jazz menu for relaxation in case a novel doesn't do it. I unfold the airline blanket and remind myself that the next trip I should bring my own, and especially a scarf or shawl for keeping my neck and shoulders warm. The neck pillow has been tossed out in my case. I don't like it, although it seems popular with the younger set along with the eye mask.

The usual flight pre safety checks commence, and I tighten my seatbelt as a matter of habit. I note the exit nearest me, and the one behind. I turn off my cell phone and contact to the outside world is shut down.

0077 pushes back from the jetway and begins its taxiway to line up for take-off. My anticipation increases the closer we get to the runway. It can't be helped, but along with the pilot going through his warm-up checklist, I am rattling off my own list of clothing and personal supplies in my suitcase.

A surging rush of adrenalin comes over me while timing the takeoff down the runway with the second hand on my watch. I feel the exact moment of liftoff.

Wheels-up signal. The flight has officially begun.

I plan to settle in for a night of tossing and turning once the plane levels-off.

Wrong.

The next thing that I know is that light is streaming in the windows and the flight attendant is serving breakfast —a cold croissant that missed the tender efforts of microwave magic, accompanied by inexcusable weak coffee.

Touchdown.

I gather up my belongings and do the same drill in reverse only it doesn't take as long, or so it appears.

No jet lag. What an amazing, wonderful way for beginning the trip. On previous flights, I have dreaded those first few hours of headaches and nauseousness while fighting to stay awake until after dinner.

If I snored and drooled on 26E's plaid shirt, so be it. That's economy class for you, up close and personal.

After going through customs and immigration into Northern Ireland, I head toward the exit where I will pick up my tour.

"You must be Kay," says the tour guide looking at the gold nametag hanging around my neck. I move in closer with my luggage, which fortunately shows up from Rochester.

I am Kay once more, and ready for a full day of sightseeing in Belfast, Ireland, the first stay on a three - week trip in the Emerald Isle. I'll leave the flight behind in my mind, and I won't give it a second thought until I am ready to pull out my return ticket.

As I leave the terminal, I throw my temporary existence as 26D in the trash.

Planting My Feet on the Soil

Green upon green upon layers of green is what my roving eyes first take in leaving the Belfast International Airport for a visit to the true Ireland away from the commercialization, gray cement slabs and signage around a transportation center too often the quick and sole view of a country on a layover. The balmy early morning breezes exude warmth, and rather unusually so, for Northern Ireland. The angle of the sun peeping above the shadows of the control tower is an invitation announcing my arrival whereby I unbutton my tightly done-up jacket hiding my tired travel shirt. I am expecting dreary; instead, I receive a glorious gift from the Irish. All the signs are here for an excellent twenty-one days.

An Irish Sunday

Settling in Peacefully to Belfast's Troubles

Too long a sacrifice
Can make a stone of the heart. — W.B. Yeats

My computer is lagging two steps behind the rest of
the cyber world. It's as slow as the non-existent foot
traffic in the lobby of the Europa Hotel. The overhead
clock states that it is 7 a.m., which is all well and good;
however, my internal body clock is rushing to play catch-
up. Not so for my computer.

I am alone on the royal blue couch except for the
solitary desk clerk finishing paperwork leftover from the
night before. The slightest shuffle of paper ruffles the air
currents, and it agitates the room's serenity as if
amplified by Saturday night's piano bar on the second
floor mezzanine. The cleaning crew is awakening today's
agenda board with a mopping of the tile floor and the
daily dusting of the pale purple hibiscus floral
arrangement prominent in the center. All the room's
design converges at this focal point.

The waft of a fresh bouquet of detergent swishes and swirls in patches surrounding me in anticipation of a brand new morn like my head wide open for exploration on my first full day in Northern Ireland.

I focus back to the computer screen. Force of habit requires me to follow my usual morning drill as if I were at my office desk — email, online newspapers and Facebook. It's six hours earlier at home as I am leaving my news on family and friends' servers. They will pick it up after I am halfway through the day.

***

I am told from my travel documents that Belfast is a robust northern metropolis of nearly half a million people. It is a scenic city situated between the waters of Belfast Lough, the Belfast Hills and the forested slopes of Cave Hill.

Belfast was the catalyst of the industrial revolution in Ulster, and specialized in the development of such industries like linen, rope making and shipbuilding with the world's largest dry dock.

The city's Victorian heritage can be seen in the stately buildings of the area around the Europa Hotel and at Belfast's Grand Opera House.

***

It could be the tracking system is off on my computer as if it sanctifies the political upheavals over forty years ago that are shrouded in oranges and greens. I give up, close the lid and go to my next plan. I have a half hour before the breakfast room is ready for guests.

The main street of Belfast is reasonably empty, but it is Sunday morning and last evening The Lion's Gate Pub was in high glee no doubt leaving its revelers a desire for a few daylight hours of respite and recovery. Robinson's is shut up tightly like a clam. Brennan's lights are off, although the front door is swinging back and forth for a couple young lads who are hauling in full kegs of beer.

I take it as my cue to get in sharp picture taking of the nearby surroundings without the encumbrance of pedestrians. I walk out into a gloriously sunny day with the temperature already warm for an early June hour, and look up and down the street seeing the city through the lens of my camera.

***

The mossy green piled-high metal trashcan along the curb with memories of yesterday's messiness is imposing on a neat uncluttered sidewalk. Click.

The ornate black window ledge on the overhang from the dark red brick building next to the hotel beckons attention to its architectural design. Click.

The elderly Sunday walker with his newspaper under his arm wrapped in its print like a special edition turns the corner with military precision. Click.

The octagon street sign on the opposite identifying a left-side traffic flow pattern moves me to look right, then left. Click.

***

The Europa Hotel is the most fashionable place I will be staying the whole trip until the last few days in Dublin's international district near the U.S. Embassy. The Europa, often given the title of the most bombed hotel in Europe dating back to The Troubles, has been redone and is a cosmopolitan center, except my only way of getting on Wi-Fi is finding an empty couch in the lobby to connect to the world... my own computer troubles, and pale in comparison to the misery suffered by the Loyalists and the social reformers in the 70s.

I return to the lobby and by magic, the area is filling rapidly with hotel guests as if a curtain has lifted and the action is resuming in a British Commonwealth city historically rich that abruptly halts by years of strife. Tourists are visiting once again,and not fearing for their safety from bombs exploding and rolling them out of their hotel beds in the middle of the night.

My touring friends get off the elevator, and we head to the breakfast room chattering about the endless possibilities in this harmonious city once the daily front-page headline around the world.

It is wise if my computer remains silent like the ghosts of Bernadette Devlin and Bobby Sands long gone to their reward as vibrant orators for the cause. It will be just fine indeed.

Rainy Days Don't Get the Irish Down

I am warned before leaving home. In Ireland I see incidences repeatedly. People give in to rain graciously and don't make a big deal over it.

No matter how an Irish day appears when looking up to the sky, somewhere a cloud cover is rolling in for the start of a drizzle. It goes away, and life goes on. I have a new appreciation for rain thanks to the Irish.

The dark umbrella wages a ferocious fight with the wind. It loses at the street corner when a gust of wind picks it up and turns it inside out only to have streams of rain pour down like kittens and puppies.

The Irish teen dressed in her short flouncy skirt and stacked heels gives up the struggle and runs across the Belfast avenue to her destination.

I wonder where she is heading in the middle of an afternoon in her Sunday best. You would think that she would catch a bus or not go outside at all.

What I observe, though, more often than not, is that the Irish usually don't use umbrellas. A light jacket with a hood suffices. Or sliding up the sweater or long scarf makes a temporary head cover, too.

Young mothers push their baby prams, and the rosy-cheeked fellows and gals are no worse for the slippery ride. Wet feet and chills bringing on a cough and cold is an old wives' tale that modern women don't believe.

The hand dryer in the ladies' room in the Dublin Art Museum is working overtime getting long hair presentable once more before heading off to appreciate art on a crowded Sunday afternoon in the galleries.

At Kylemore Abbey in the Connemara region of Galway, hundreds of international tourists are visiting the Gothic mansion, Victorian gardens and chapel during a steady downpour, which hasn't dampened their spirits.

I hardly see through the sheets of rain as I determine to appreciate my surroundings realizing that I may never be here again in my lifetime. It's a definite Irish reality check in looking on the bright side of things while peering out from my hood's obstructed view. I do note that most people are laughing and taking in the sights dressed in their appropriate gear.

It's not a chilly cold, rather one of those days reminding me of childhood afternoons walking through the puddles purposefully for the fun of it empty of thoughts for a brief moment away from adults.

Returning to the hotel, I peel off the outer layers and hang them to dry. Thank goodness for wicking, waterproof clothing … and big purses, too, for protecting my camera. Travel books and previous visitors alerted me to packing the right necessities.

Speaking of photography, cloudy days are best for pictures and they bring out the fullest in a scene. I capitalize on that and find pasturelands exquisite in their mist and shadows. One quick shot of a thatched roof cottage in the pouring rain illuminates reflective pinks and blues. It's priceless without any words accompanying it.

The question to myself in Ireland each morning: Do I bring the light raincoat, umbrella or take my chances? I give up listening to Irish TV and the BBC for the forecasters are so optimistic, along with being the wittiest commentators on earth. I don't know what's in store except "a chance of rain."

The half-full or half-empty theory works well. "It's a warm, sunny day with occasional showers, or a showery, overcast day with occasional sunshine, depending upon your point of view," says Pete McCarthy in his travelogue of Ireland, *McCarthy's Bar*. That's from an Englishman searching his Irish roots via stopping at all pubs with his name on the signage. (This book makes a good read if you don't mind the English humor poking at tourists, especially idiosyncratic American habits.)

Apparently, McCarthy makes it through a lot of dreary days in pubs and engages with the local folks in their desire to be hospitable and humorous while tipping their pints. Ireland's ability to absorb newcomers should never be underestimated.

No wonder the art of storytelling and music as a rich cultural heritage is so prominent. Long winter nights, damp days and lack of sunlight put thoughts into words for the reflective soul. There is a readymade audience for a well-told tale at the local pub before the music kicks in later on.

In Ireland the unexpected happens more often than not. That includes the rain. They've come to terms with it, and you hardly hear an Irishman discuss it, other than apologizing for the weather to tourists.

Late one afternoon, I went to a supermarket. The weather had had its ups and downs… mostly on the negative side, and I was tired.

"It's been an Irish sort of day," the supermarket checker tells me handing over my purchase. He pauses. He looks carefully. He waits for my reply.

I can't let him down. I'm obligated to give a clever answer.

"Tomorrow it will sprinkle sunshine," I tell him.

We laugh a hearty laugh, and a bond is formed. The Irish and I are on the same wavelength about the weather.

A little of that positive Irish attitude could go miles— well, inches — in stretching the rain gauge's capacity at home, too.

Walking the Peace Bridge

Londonderry, Northern Ireland

The silver bridge spanning the River Foyle is cloaked in early morning fog. It is about two blocks from the City Hotel Derry. I photograph it rather unsuccessfully from the parking lot dodging cars pulling in and out of the few marked vehicle spots close to the hotel's main entrance. Twenty years ago it would have been bullets.

Occasionally you can't see things clearly until years later when blurring of the edges subsides and the full wide-screened view is available for sharper contemplation.

> *Let there be peace on earth*
> *The peace that was meant to be.*

The angle is wrong for a picture as if I can't be naively simplistic about Irish life wagging my finger at the right and wrong of it. Repeatedly, one object or another is in the way of the viewfinder. I give up and take it in with my eyes instead respectfully considering what issue is debated so heatedly that causes mothers' tears dropping like bloodshed on the street. On the other side in the "Troubles" is not so far in the distance of my adulthood memory.

With God as our father

brothers all are we

Let me walk with my brother

in perfect harmony.

Twenty years ago, why even ten years ago, it was risky to visit Londonderry. A waving orange flag marks a clear territorial stake; or the red, white and blue British Commonwealth flag signals where the loyalty resides at this doorstep. The flags are displayed in neighborhoods today, along with the American flag, in honor of our willingness to assist with the settling of the truce.

Which pub to enter, and which one to stay out of, is of upmost importance, as no doubt I could be pulled into a heated discussion all one-sided. Not so anymore. This afternoon I will select a pub at random on a side street, and the owner, barkeep and the other patrons will greet me graciously for I am a tourist, and Derry folk love American visitors.

The walking and cycling bridge is open since 2011 and the hill on the opposite side is home to mostly working class Catholics. Slowly, a memorial park is being added along with a museum to record the historical implications.

I am a true believer that as in a marriage it takes two to tango, and likewise in conflict and subsequent peace, there must be dialogue and trust among rivaling sides. Over and over folks mention in tour lectures that I am not to consider this as Protestant vs. Catholic, but it is over social conditions that are not equal for all. The fact that the poorer and more needy are the Catholic families is not to make it a religious war as erroneously recorded in the history books.

Furthermore, I am a supporter of peace and peaceful solutions. Man builds walls to protect himself from his enemies and he assumes he is safer within the walls. What about the human beings that God created that live outside the walls by no fault of their birth and condition? Are they the "enemy?"

"You can't separate peace from freedom because no one can be at peace unless he has freedom." – Malcolm X

Just by my own nature, I feel like a kid that wants on the other side and is forbidden to go. Yet it is safe and not forbidden fruit anymore.

After a full day of touring my legs are ready to be stretched horizontal, I know that I must make the half mile walk and envelop the serenity within the spans that now shadows all the turmoil of the past. I must be part of the experience, inch-by-inch feeling the gray sky lift and the late afternoon sun poke out signaling the safety of the journey.

Two Irish hotel maids in their uniforms bustle past me with their canvass totes in hand hurrying home no doubt to start dinner and cleaning all over again in their own places up on the hillside. They engage in quick bits of conversation all in a day's work.

It is not a long walk at all, and my step lightens and my energy renews when I look back at my hotel on the other side of the riverbank now with flickering lights popping on here and there at day's end.

I lean on the rough stonewall and brush my hand over its imperfections. Things haven't always been so smooth in my life, but I have survived like the people of this fair city in the northern lands. Perhaps, we are both in respite for the time being. May it be so.

Let peace begin with me

Let this be the moment now.
With every step I take

Let this be my solemn vow.
To take each moment

And live each moment

With peace eternally.
Let there be peace on earth,
And let it begin with me.
Jill Jackson Miller and Sy Miller

Seamus Heaney, A Modern Irish Soul

Londonderry, Northern Ireland

Londonderry is the birthplace of poet Seamus Heaney, whom many consider a later day Yeats. He is an easy portal for me into the contemporary culture of Erin. Struggling with Yeats can be tiring and often enigmatic even though I do so appreciate his work.

How ironic that Heaney passes away late this summer after I return from my visit. A touch of sadness hands my journey a somber tone in a deep bass key. My thoughts cry his flowing passages like droplets of ink still wet on the page. They are such expressive words of everything Irish, especially the landscapes left in my mind.

We have no prairies
To slice a big sun at evening—
Everywhere the eye conceded to
Encroaching horizon,
IS wooded from the cyclops' eye
Of a tarn. Our unfenced country
Is bog that keeps crusting
Between the sights of the sun.
"Bogland"— Seamus Heaney

Inside. Outside. All around the town from the walled protected old city established by the Scotch Protestant to the homes and businesses, primarily owned by the Irish Catholics along the river, describes modern day, Derry, or Londonderry, depending on your history.

Londonderry is situated on a picturesque hillside on the banks of the Foyle Estuary. Founded by St. Columba in the sixth century, this is the fourth-largest city on the island of Ireland and is known today for the vitality of its cultural life.

There is a full day of touring and it starts with a walking tour inside the walls dating from the 17th century that encircle Londonderry's historic center.

The Tower Museum exhibits the maritime history of Londonderry, and the Guildhall built in 1890 in the Gothic architectural style, similar to its London counterpart. Austin's Department Store is the oldest one in Northern Ireland and is majestic in style with the rest of the older city.

I don't remember sighting a place marker identifying a Heaney residence, although I will find a residence in Dublin later. Part of his spirit rests in Londonderry along with the influence of the times. If nothing more, it reminds me to continue reading his poetry. As a poet from Northern Ireland, Heaney uses his work to reflect upon the "Troubles," the often-violent political struggles that plagued the country during Heaney's young adulthood. The poet seeks to weave the ongoing Irish troubles into a broader historical frame embracing the general human situation.

The rain is determined to be persistent and will drench me most of the day while at the Ulster American Folk Park tour.

Cloudburst and steady downpour now for days.
"The Gifts of Rain" — Seamus Heaney

The Park tells the story of the immigration from Ulster to America in the 18th and 19th centuries and provides visitors with a "living history" experience on its outdoor site. Costumed guides and craftspeople recreate the past in an outdoor museum that includes a weaver's cottage, forge, schoolhouse, log cabin, church and a 19th century Ulster street.

For no particular reason, rain or not, I feel the urge to walk the paths that my camera guides me to for visual stimulation, and I forgo the inside museum of historical Irish immigration. I believe that I will learn more on the walk. The fresh air and chilly temperatures are more appealing than thinking about being stuffed into a small windowless cabin for a voyage across the sea to America.

Fortunately for my camera lens I have the acreage relatively to myself. It's a simple picture-taking afternoon, and I download several of my best trip shots at the hotel in the evening. There are "gifts" that come in the rain to make me grateful.

I'll Tip a Pint to Friendship

What's a woman to do when she has specific requests from everybody and his brother before leaving home? Tip a pint for good luck and nod in their honor. I have no other choice as I dearly love my friends and acquaintances, and do the obvious—belly up to the Londonderry bar one mid-afternoon and ask for a pint on tap.

But, I discover that it isn't all that simple. Not being much of a barfly anymore, I don't even know the choices back in the states for reference. (Yes, I should have done better research on this particular topic.) I am puzzled as what to order in the beer category.

To err on the safe side and attempt not to appear so naive, I ask the barmaid to make the selection for me, and she nods willingly sharing her expertise by questioning my likes and dislikes all with a patient Irish smile on her face. Light? Ale? I tell her that I have been satisfied with dark beer that is full-bodied in the past. She understands what I don't about the characteristics of brew, and she pours me a pint of Guinness Stout. Sláinte.

Unfinished Business

If you ever go across the sea to Ireland
Then maybe at the closing of your day
You will sit and watch the moon rise over Claddagh
And see the sun go down on Galway Bay.
Dr. Arthur Colahan

I don't like the notion of leaving Galway. There are too many immediate experiences that I want to keep reliving, and I prefer staying stuck in a 33 and one-third rpm vinyl record groove. I lift the arm and reposition the needle carefully back a bit on the record for another listen to Patrick O'Dea's tenor voice.

Galway is a little bit bohemian within a relaxing, musical city, and I am caught up in the exhilaration bursting from the atmosphere. I have lost track of how many times I have taken the now familiar shuttle bus from the hotel to the city center for just one more discovery like the kid fitting together the old Lego pieces into a new construction surprising himself immensely.

Record players. Tape recorders. iTunes. It doesn't matter. They all perform the identical function.

Pause.

Replay the taste of the fresh-caught salmon dinner at the restaurant overlooking the bay — an Irish ceili (an Irish celebration of the harvest) of hearty food, followed by song, dance and story way past my normal bedtime. It's my first opportunity to watch two young costumed Irish dancers close up, and they put on quite a remarkable performance. After I observe them out of the corner of my eye heading out the backdoor, checking their text messages before driving away. Obviously, they are older than they first appear with that wide-eyed innocent look on the wooden platform stage, but perhaps that is part of their performance for travelers — entertaining an illusion of the old Ireland.

Replay the Saturday afternoon stroll to the tunes of one set of performers to another carrying me among throngs of people down the historic winding cobblestone streets up from the River Corrib. To the left and to the right, pubs in wooden buildings dating back into the past are packed to overflowing, spilling merrymakers onto the streets. They're getting a head start it would appear for the hour of dusk is nowhere near. I have to firmly navigate around groups of folks stopped to chat to get in doorways to stores. I don't mind as it gives a festive air to my day. Finally, I settle for the English teashop where a group of my traveling companions meet for high tea at four o'clock with proper cucumber sandwiches and Irish Barry's Tea.

Replay my visit to Dubray Books and discover Irish author, Kevin Barry. There is an interview with Barry on Irish News in the morning, and from what little I hear and the interviewer's personal recommendation, I decide to search for his book. It seems the right thing to do to buy the $1Euro recyclable blue tote to hold my purchase, especially because there is a quote from W.B. Yeats on it: *"Take down this book and slowly read..."*

Bookstores do it to me every single time. There is an energy that builds up within me. I have to force myself to leave the shelves upon shelves of Irish books to meet a friend at a little restaurant on a compact side street for Irish stew and soda bread, a staple of my diet and my comfort food only a week into my trip.

Replay my adventure into a Galway supermarket to find Irish tea and talk, with one after another of the helpful clerks up and down the aisles like I am a local with news to spread. It doesn't matter to them, or me. A little curiosity goes a long way, and the prices of different products will be a conversational topic at home, along with any glimpse into the life of a working person in Galway that I can glean.

Replay the luncheon cruise on Killary, a charming fjord. My usual seasickness anytime I travel over an hour on a boat does not happen for some reason, and I am relieved. Again, I select the salmon over mashed potatoes like a broken record too delicious to forego. Unfortunately, we are shrouded in fog and I have no clue as to the land and water connecting together, but if the scene is replayed, then the weather will be grand.

Replay the ride along the coast catching sight of the famine homes as shells of themselves and feeling overwhelmed at the starvation and crying coming from thin air, like I am there when the last person shuts the door before the New World. A tear is shed, an outward glimpse into my somber mood while reliving the disruption of a little Irish lass leaving all behind except for the dirty rag doll clutched in her arm. The miles and miles of stonewall in every direction still divide the land as the heart is softening. In recent time, so many youth have immigrated depleting Ireland of its workforce. Those that remain are trying to make a go of it in small town businesses as risky as their pals who have gone to Australia and Canada.

Record.

My fine-tuned business is repeated and complete in Galway. The memories are stored in my brain forever to bring to the front whenever I so desire.

Play forward. On to Killarney.

Places Where Thoughts Grow

The wedding knot is tied at 6 p.m. in a solemn Catholic mass draped in the robes of Irish reverence. Immediately after the priest introduces the new couple and invites the bride and groom to kiss as husband and wife, the somber mood lifts and everyone traipses up the street in high glee to the Tower Hotel for the gala reception.

***

Ireland has been both pensive and boisterous since the beginning of its settlement, and there are no signs that it won't continue balancing the two diametrically opposite societal mores through future generations. The quietness of a listener deep into the thoughts of another soul, and the raucous nature of the same Irishman with a twinkle in his eye relishing life's simplicities, remains deeply entrenched in the fine art of conversation.

The lonely shepherd working the pastoral countryside who becomes an energetic storyteller weaving tales in the lively pub in the eve, remain back-to-back aspects of an Irishman's daily life.

And may the thoughts of Ireland brood
Upon a measured quietude.
"To Ireland in the Coming Times" — W.B. Yeats

***

Early one foggy morning in the coastal town of Waterford, famed as the original manufacturing site for the majestic glass works, The House of Waterford Crystal, I peer out my hotel picture window at the blurry harbor … and into the distant past and future.

Hardly a soul is stirring, and other than the street sweeper machine cleansing the road from yesterday's traffic, no one is noticeably strolling the graveled path by the harbor. The pavement is sparkling from the rivulets of water like the magnificent facets of hand-blown glass fashioned for decades by experienced craftsmen down the street.

I capture a perfect moment to suspend in time simply because I want to reflect in solitude the road to today's modern Waterford city.

The Vikings founded the city in AD 914, and named from a word that originally meant, "windy fjord." Like many Irish cities Waterford has gone through repeated historical upheavals. But its constancy to the crown in the face of a pretender revolt in 1497 earned it a motto that sticks to this day: Urbs Intacta Manet Waterfordia ("Waterford remains the untaken city"). Although Waterford withstood a withering siege by Oliver

Cromwell in 1649, it finally surrendered during a second attack the following year.

The city thrived in the 18th century. The glassworks, founded in 1783 by George and William Penrose, is prized the world over for the highest quality lead-cut crystal.

***

It is a noisy and restless sleeping night tossing and turning like I am pitching and rolling on a tumultuous sea during a violent storm. Scraps of a day's experiences float randomly in my mind as disjointed shards of cream porcelain pottery on the Belleek floor in County Fermanagh waiting to be mopped away.

My window overlooks Main Street under the hotel entrance marquee blinking its neon welcome. There had been a wedding celebration, which like all good family parties in Ireland, goes on and on into the wee hours spilling out on the sidewalk making room for more exuberant festivity in clusters of multi-generational folk clinking glasses and toasting young love.

The full momentum didn't get well under way until after midnight, and by then, I am fading in and out of sleep fitfully pondering my own thoughts. I truly don't mind any inconvenience for I reason that a young couple is beginning their journey, and there is no room for negative vibes to spoil the event. A second and third pillow's usefulness becomes acceptable sound deafening devices like they were positioned for that specific duty on the bed in the first place.

***

The Irish display a definite stamina when it comes to conversation and music, much more than I am used to handling. In each hotel throughout the country from Belfast to Dublin, the streets are filled with a party atmosphere every day of the week including Sunday nights. It makes no difference if my room is located facing a murky back alley or across the street from the colorful front entrance to the bookmaker's joint. Laughter erupts out of thin air like a circuit of stars on a moon struck eve. Yet, there is never a rowdy drunkenness to it for the laws on the Irish books are strictly enforced when it comes to drinking and driving.

***

When I return from visiting a rural seaside pub several miles away, the wedding reception is going strong with no signs of wilting like the yellow corsage left forgotten on a tabletop by a bridesmaid.

Young primary school boys and girls weave in and out of the banquet rooms in their glamorous little outfits and hair flying askew giggling, for they are extending their bedtimes by a long stretch. The merriment takes over the lobby's atmosphere and greets weary hotel guests checking in for a night's respite.

I laugh and head upstairs to my room knowing that tomorrow will be an early wake-up call. When the elevator door opens onto my floor, there are the bride and groom — I am assuming it is the groom, and not the best man — in their formal finery blushing while he fastens up her gown's zipper. A moment or two of quiet in the midst of spirited celebration grounds even the most exuberant and hardy social beings. But as I unlock my door, a sinking feeling drops my mood as a bad omen, which I try to push out of my head.

***

In sharp contrast is St. Columba's Parish Church at Drumcliffe in County Sligo where I stand in solemn reverence at the grave of W.B. Yeats, a poet for whom I have great affection, and I reflect on what he passes on to enhance my writing life. Such beautiful language in sparing lines of verse is the artistry of a master.

I have the spot to myself and pay my respects while the tumbling clouds of rain play tricks back and forth between the streaks of sunlight. Such is life in Ireland, and it permeates into the soulful truths of the great thinkers.

Cast a cold Eye
On Life, on Death
Horseman, pass by!. — W.B. Yeats

Few would question the fact that the man who wrote those words and asked to have them placed there was a literary genius. This genius was recognized when the Nobel Prize for Literature was awarded to W.B. Yeats in 1923. The citation stated, "For his always inspired poetry, which in highly artistic form gives expression to the spirit of a whole nation"

Not the most popular tourist attraction by a long stretch, the bucolic cemetery and I are left to our own inspirations. Its stonework is laced together with ivy creeping quietly up and down to frame the ironwork gate to heaven. Graves of heavy slabs set flat into the ground are adorned with a few wild white daisies popping up here and there. Larger upright headstones with scripted history of lives etched into the stone mark a Protestant churchyard bereft of crosses and crucifixes of the Catholic sort.

Looking around at the sloping land and rolling hills with Ben Bulben Mountain in the distance, it all is good I remark to the wind. Simplicity and contentment make it a place for final rest. The sheep, grazing on nearby hillsides in a plethora of gradations of green, affirm my declaration like the God of Glory from above.

Tread softly
because you tread on
my dreams. — W.B. Yeats

The intense natural beauty of Ireland, especially in the rugged coast of the west, is way beyond my wildest expectations. No photograph in any travel book does it the justice it deserves. I look and look everywhere and relish places for the sheer joy of my feet touching the Irish soil lifting its beauty into my heart to carry with me forever.

I stand in awe of surreal moonscape full of huge limestone crags rather than bogs and pastures of the interior region. Scanning the horizon I wonder at the inhospitable setting and how plants thrive, or in fact, how do people thrive?

Perhaps, a writer's brooding in his aloneness of the place cultivates ample material for a novel or poem when the darkened days of winter occur over and over shading and shaping words. A single rock surfacing in low tide framed in the shimmer of the sun's rising is the means for a writer to get into his head and undo years of complex ideas.

A shoulder of rock
Sticks high up of the sea
"High Island" — Richard Murphy

When I return home I read about the modern poet, Richard Murphy, who was born in County Mayo in a rural setting and teaches in American universities. His work exemplifies the draw of one's homeland. His poems are contemporary manifestations of historical events challenging the Irish with their unfenced land bordered by the sea and often exploited by their enemies.

***

All is not well the morning after for the newlyweds in Waterford. Gossip amongst the wait staff whispering within earshot of my table at breakfast has it the couple is getting an annulment, and it is not meant to be happily ever after for them together.

My tablemates and I share mixed assumptions while we are served our hot Irish oatmeal and assorted sausage and bacon. The time and effort into one event goes "poof" in the night like a firefly here and then disappears into the darkness to come out again in glorious splendor in the appropriate moment on life's journey. I leave the table with a few lingering sober thoughts that I will process in the days to come.

***

Yeats writes how 'Love fled', reminding me to take a step back from the gaiety and grab hold of life's pattern of reality for good or bad accepting its subtle moments. Shades of despair last as long one permits, and the Irish are a resilient folk, the potato famine speaks well to that. And the wedding of last evening that comes unraveled as trails of lonely strands of wool separate into pieces.

Life is mine to embrace in agreement with the bold ideas of 'the red-rose bordered hem' of Ireland, before the beginning of time. Thanks be to W.B. Yeats and his universal language for all mankind. The contemporary poets from Ireland cast a similar glow on the richness of the people and their place where abundant life is within the mind.

An Irish Sunday

Caving in to the Cliffs of Moher Triumphantly

Today I put on
A terrible strength
Invoking the Trinity,
Confessing the Three
With faith in the One
As I face my Maker.
Anonymous — Eighth century Irish Bard

The early morning mist is in my eyes hindering my heart from experiencing clearly the full measure of nature's beauty stretching out in front. Soaking it in is to be out of focus like the blurring of the windowpane from the humidity of a coastal day's fickle weather.

Halfway through the three weeks, I wake up sad on a Sunday morning. Up until then, I kept patting myself on the back and reinforcing my worrisome nature. "I am doing well on my own and taking it all in stride." I am exhausted from the overabundant sensory experiences that are pouring into my soul and flooding my deepest cavity. For the first time in my life, I am scared because words are not coming to put the thoughts down on paper.

I am letting go the fight and dropping the journal to the bottom of my luggage. Perhaps I need extended space to my own reveries without the other folks on the bus offering their own versions of the scenery moderating mine. And too, I am missing my usual travel partner.

All I know is that I ache, and I become a mere robot packing my belongings for the move from Galway to Killarney, eating breakfast mindlessly and studying the prescribed agenda for the day glad that I don't have to make any travel decisions.

I am distressed when I hike up the path to see the Cliffs of Moher. All the chatter going on around me reverberates in chorus, "alone, alone," and everyone except for me is part of a couple. Pity is engulfing in waves over me splashing morosely over my body. I should be alive and alert. I am not.

**

The majestic Cliffs of Moher are precipitous rock formations — towering over 700 feet above the crashing ocean surf at their highest point — that offer breathtaking panoramic views of Ireland's Atlantic coast. These magnificent cliffs provide nesting sites for tens of thousands of seabirds. If the wind is strong, the sea spray and foam flies up and over the cliffs along with the rain; while on clear sunny days, fantastic views can be seen from every angle.

Over the centuries, people have also made their mark, with towers, quarries, well-worn paths, but they are lost in the grandeur of the sea cliffs.

***

I do the proper touristy photographic duty taking pictures for others, and I have my own done in return, but reticently: the signature smile on my face that people at home have since remarked is a fake one. I am depressed in the gloom and doom of my thoughts pulling me inward inventing mammoth problems that are not of my choosing.

I walk and walk up the many steps reaching all the excellent vantage points for viewing looking beyond the immediate and out into the past and future of my existence. How much longer will I be walking this earth? I rest my weathered hand with newly done nails on the edge of the rough wall and turn away from the cliffs peering into the distant sky. It is not a thought I want to wrestle in my head, and I sigh. I let it go in hopeful expectation and continue hiking to the top of the walkway as if my pilgrimage spirals to the pearly gates.

There is to be a rude awakening of my soul snapping me back into the flow of the tour. It isn't anything extraordinary, and more on the simpler order of living organisms, that catches my attention. A three-inch yellow flower is sticking out of one of the crevices in the rock. A beautiful delicate flower in a harsh landscape of grays and whites is standing up tall inviting me to detect its serenity and peace poised all alone fearlessly far away from any other plant. That does it. Here I am in my yellow raincoat standing out in all my completeness of character functioning well. I thank the humble solitary flower for its lesson, and I continue to the visitor's center in a much relieved and accepting frame of mind.

Like a capricious fairy in the hedgerows, my mind plays tricks keeping the magical dusting of joy a little far out of my hand's reach. That is the conclusion that I come to as the bus journeys on to our hotel in Killarney. Negative spells will plague me for a brief moment, and engaging in solitary soul searching I will get my equilibrium.

Through my veiled eyes, I take in all there is of the Cliffs of Moher from a different perspective, and to this day I smell the ocean's saltiness and dampness in my brown limp curls symbolizing the vast power the senses have over my being.

The Elusive Irish Shamrock

I wake up this morning realizing that I must take a new tactic — hang my head down more instead of looking all around me. I should be searching for a four-leaf clover, an Irish shamrock no less, bringing it home and pressing it between the pages of an Edna O' Brien novel. It will serve as a natural unspoken reminder of the stretches of creativity in Ireland throughout the ages and a connection between written words of a more recent generation. My noble plan is never to happen. Instead, I bring back light black rocks from the edge of Galway Bay. They serve as a stone's throw to the well-worn collection of books on my shelf.

No Kissing, Thank You Very Much

"The real voyage of discovery consists not in seeking new landscapes but in having new eyes." – Marcel Proust

    I haven't stepped one foot down off the tour bus before a delicate conversation begins around me. I am using the word, "delicate" lightly here. This is one of a personal nature, and frankly, no one's business.

    The line of thirty-five men and women pass miniscule bits of conversation back and forth like the old toy telephone gossip game that messes up any reasonable piece of news forever. It isn't gossip, though. Who is, and who isn't doing it — kissing the Blarney Stone — is next on our afternoon's agenda. There are the "yes" people, and the definite "no" people, along with a few of us that are riding outside the wall so to speak. I leave it at that for I want to take in the situation before I decide. Actually, I don't believe that it will matter one way or another in my book of accomplishments that I will leave behind. And if you think that the height scares me, well, no way. You don't know me then.

I hear buzz about concerns over sanitation—how many sweet smooches already will have left their imprint by high noon? How difficult it might be leaning way over, help or no help, bracing a fragile back. The cost keeps factoring into the talk that is now breaking off between smaller groups as we exit the bus. I notice how our tour guide, Gus, conveniently gets out of our way and leaves us wondering what to do like a wise parental figure.

***

Blarney Castle has a 129-step staircase leading to a tower to the famed "Blarney Stone. According to legend, anyone who manages the backward lean to kiss it receives the "gift of gab" — a smooth, soothing way with words that best mean nothing.

The word "blarney" was coined by Elizabeth I to describe her endless and fruitless discussions with Dermot McCarthy over his surrender of the castle to the Crown.

The McCarthys built the present castle with its 85-foot-high keep in 1446, replacing an earlier castle. Though the Blarney Stone gets all the publicity, the castle's tower house and surrounding gardens are superb in their own right. The grounds also include caves, dungeons and a rock garden of ancient trees and weathered stones.

***

My first sighting of Blarney Castle runs chills down my spine, and a few of those ice cubes would certainly help with the oppressive Irish heat that breaks out to honor our visit. I am learning by now to live like the Irish and not get in the way of a gift of warm weather from Mother Nature.

The castle is every bit like I imagine with its sturdy gray stone sides and keep looming high in the perfectly still blue sky. It would be a paradise for thoughts if it weren't for a frenzy of tourists pushing and shoving up and down the footpaths like streams of ants marching to war. I'm in my sensible sneakers and dark pants with a checkered short-sleeve shirt to add a bit of color. The walkway up the hill to the castle is lined with seasonal flowers, and once again the Irish roses win all the awards in my book. The lovely yellows and shades of pink offset the dark greenways groomed immaculately by the gardeners. The gardens cover over sixty acres of sprawling parklands.

If I had the place to myself, I would live the dream of strolling as the duchess of Blarney Castle in my long billowy gold threaded gown waiting for the duke and his knights to return from the battlefield. All of my children would be freely frolicking about after their tutoring lessons in the morning that held them inside. This late afternoon a rider appears with a message, and soon the thin line of weary soldiers come back to the castle to regroup. There will be rowdy merriment and feasting way into the morning hours in celebration while my fluttering eyelids droop in response. Ah, my duke is home, even for a few hours.

People are doing their stint at the castle before crossing the bridge into the town for a longer visit to the numerous shops and restaurants that have sprung up to keep people spending tourist dollars all in one spot. There is no waiting them out. I continue upward and onward.

I am most impressed by the stone staircase, and my decision will be to have a go at what awaits at the top level. Inch by inch I step up on the uneven stairs worn down by untold number of visitors—generations of residents, too — ahead of me through the centuries. There are lookout openings in the wall, and a drift of breeze is welcome relief. At one point I realize there is no turning around, and I continue at the slow pace set by others. The petty conversation on the way up is more of the complaining and whining nature over useless things with no solutions, and I tune it out as best as possible. Instead, I recall climbing lighthouses at brisk paces without giving it a thought in younger years, and with no one pushing me along either, to view the Great Lakes or Atlantic Ocean. Achieving the climbing goal appears to be on everyone's mind.

I make it in good shape. Arriving on the top wall, I check what the situation at the stone is all about, and discover that more than one or two people are passing it by with a wave of the hand.

Every third or fourth person deposits their glasses and purses on the ground, turns backward, is let down gently with hands of skilled helpers and — I am blocked by the crowd in front of me from seeing this part—kisses the Blarney Stone. Over in just a mere thirty seconds and another soul is blabbering away with the gift of gab.

It's not for me, and I offer no apologies. I wind my way back down the stairway and come to the bottom of the castle near the moat. There's an hour left, and perhaps, if I turn this corner by the creek, I might blot out the noise, confusion and human beings. The lawn looks ever so inviting.

It is here behind the castle battlements that I find the Poison Garden. This part of the grounds contrasts largely with the bright green scenes everywhere else in the grounds. The poisonous plants from around the world, including ones from Harry Potter like the Wolfsbane and the Mandrake, are clearly labeled with information for modern day viewers.

"The truth is that the Irish are so clear-headed and critical that they still regard rhetoric as a distinct art, as the ancients did. Thus a man makes a speech as a man plays a violin, not necessarily without feeling, but chiefly because he knows how to do it. Another instance of the same thing is that quality which is always called the Irish charm. The Irish are agreeable, not because they are particularly emotional, but because they are very highly civilised. Blarney is a ritual; as much of a ritual as kissing the Blarney Stone." — GK Chesterton

Echoing Cork City's Delights

"Wandering re-establishes the original harmony which once existed between man and the universe." — Anatole France

Two hours to myself is exactly what I require to seek out an impromptu adventure on foot, one of those forever memories that makes a tourist into a traveler.

There's a difference in my estimation, when one is able to be
 absorbed into the culture of the present: to capture the meaning of life for the common good. To be transported far from the tour bus or train's chatter that comes straight out of the universal travel guide's page.

There's no agenda. There's no outcome other than to be enveloped into the beat of everyman on the street and take up my walking stick tapping spritely along as if a leprechaun is hanging on to the childlike wonder of it all.

Cork, Ireland's second-largest city is where I am staying at the Imperial Hotel on Oliver Plunkett Street, a shabby chic high-rise soon to be razed in favor of more retail buildings lining the South Mall. Oh, my. It's best that I am visiting now, as I can't imagine having to stay in a suburban chain hotel a distance out of the older part of the city—European city centers hold special pedestrian charm — contending with the onslaught of traffic at every intersection, overpriced taxi fares and indecipherable tram schedules.

The minute I step out the revolving door and onto the pavement, I am lifted into the movement of throngs of people rushing to unknown destinations. The weather is balmy, and it is comfortable for a change providing ample visibility here and there without the obstructed view from behind a coat's hood.

I head north to the main avenue through several back streets far removed from the narrow medieval lanes of earlier history where a damsel in her long fitted gown stepping ever so gingerly on the cobblestones in high laced boots avoiding the sludge and runoff of life's embarrassing necessities, might be a commonplace figure on the commercial scene.

Getting lost is not one of my worries; and in fact, it could provide me with the perfect opportunity for seeking out Irish folks to engage with in conversation like has happened by chance over and over on this trip.

Quaint tiny postcard-size boutiques filled with toiletries, perfumes and soaps don't attract my attention beyond window-shopping. They are placed here and there between pubs sprawling with younger folks seated at outside umbrella-covered tables in clusters of twos and threes chatting up the latest gossip with no other cares in the world. I float in and out of bits and pieces of dialogue…"How's the weather suiting you?"…"Where is dinner tonight?"…"My job is…"in the lilting voices that I have come to appreciate as sincere warm tonal blends like a smooth hot Irish coffee with a puff of whipped cream on a summer's afternoon.

There is one colorful place with its checkered outside paint trim that beckons me. It has high-end women's fashions sparingly placed on pink cloth-covered hangers in a nook of a store I am hardly able to navigate for fear my purse will nudge silken gowns   sliding to the floor while I hang my head in embarrassment. At home when I enter such a store, I know instantly that I should do an about face and leave before the sales clerk gives me that uppity look telling me I am out of my element and price range.

Not so here. The Irish are eager merchants and know that tourist dollars keep them afloat in difficult times. An elegantly dressed shop girl wearing an outfit of sheer blue print with lacy full sleeves greets me cordially and invites me to take my time looking over the latest fashions.

My hand sweeps through the rack of linen tops until it rests on a rust colored tunic with tiny stitching running down the front. It is gorgeous and would be smashing with linen pants. Lovely. The Euros price tag is written in tiny print as if one who wants it doesn't have to check the price.

My adrenalin surges upward on the metered scale of shopping, and I now feel that more of the same is what the doctor orders. It won't be in this establishment, but I am mentally set. I leave waving goodbye and thank her for a moment of her time.

I turn into the English Market, noted for its huge selection of fresh produce, with my eye out to buy the most delicious Irish cheese that I might find. Two travel friends from Oregon and I will collect in one of our hotel rooms for wine, cheese and crackers this evening, and I want to bring a specialty that I can brag on along with the tale of where I found it like playing a scavenger hunt game with myself.

The cheese lady is straight ahead, and I listen as she explains her choices with their unique tastes. I sample a couple before picking the Irish mild cheddar made locally. She tells me that when I return home, I should look for cheese from specific regions such as Dublin or Cork, as that will be how the cheddars and Gruenin are labeled.

A quick circle through the rest of the indoor market shows that boxed strawberries are in season, duck eggs are popular and fresh fish from today's catch is ready to be weighed, wrapped in newspaper and sold. Shoppers are rushing from booth to booth clutching cloth shopping bags of various sizes and shapes. (I have learned in my Irish visit that plastic bags are only given out upon request, and in some cases there is a charge.)

I exit before getting too twisted around seeking the way I came in, and walk out sighting Brown Thomas Department store to the right in Cork's favorite fashion district appropriately named, Opera Lane, for it brings singing to my heart as if my internal radar is directing me faster than the speed of sound. That's where I will go to browse the floors and floors of merchandise to my content and when my feet tell me that I have had enough of scarves, dresses and jewelry, I will depart.

The wide street is filled with other tourists trying to get in their last minute fix of shopping. There is a distinct sound between all the other normal conversational melodies coming from the street corner, though. It is shouting, "Echo. Echo." I glance around me and there is a craggy old newspaper seller seated cross-legged on a low portable stool close to the ground with a stack of the Cork daily newspaper afternoon edition, *"The Echo,"* as if a reminder of the past when print was the way to get the latest information while waiting patiently on my porch for the newsboy to roll up on his bike with Long Island's *Newsday*. I stop, hand over my Euro and pick up a copy to read in the evening. He puts my coin in his front apron pocket, and the next customer adds more change almost in unison. I stand back to take it all in watching Cork residents move in and out of the seller's space until the pile of papers has decreased in a relatively short time. (When I retrace my steps past this spot in a couple hours, it is empty as if erased from the daily calendar as yesterday's news, except for the memory snapped by my camera.)

The front entrance of the department store salutes me with a tip of the hat by the doorman dressed in his finest formal attire.

In my estimation, there is nothing to compare with the atmosphere of a busy department store with aisle after aisle piled high in merchandise, and in this locale, all marked in Euros giving me an additional challenge figuring out equivalent costs in dollars. A born and bred people watcher, I learn much about culture and lifestyles observing consumers sizing up the latest styles, and even what they are wearing themselves reflecting their personal tastes. Prices intrigue me — clothing is costly — and the limited quantity is apparent.

It hardly takes a second before the ice is broken at the watch counter, and while examining the choices laid on the velvet tray with one blue-eyed sales girl, two others also with shiny jet-black hair draw in closer and listen in to my questions about the city. I want to know where the best place to go this evening for dinner, and to a spot that will have live music, too, all in a single place less touristy and more for the Cork native.

One by one the three shop girls dressed in their look alike navy blue blazers aptly tell me, "Every night there is two or three nearby pub gatherings for laughing or crying together with friends, or total strangers that feel your emotions."

They assure me that if I simply show up at the door, I will be welcome in any number of places as if I am returning back home for a family gathering. They are more than polite while I am making my purchase, and frankly, I am not expecting such open conversation showing they truly care to impart what they hold dear, along with their curiosity about an American's impressions of their country.

Retuning to the hotel, I do not have many shopping bags. Looking at the choice hours from another angle, there is much in my heart echoing for the pleasure of a couple brief hours mingling amongst the ways of the Irish.

"One's destination is never a place, but a new way of seeing things." – Henry Miller

The Irish Get It Right

First one, and then two more shop girls move over closer. We talk and talk in the busiest department store in Cork, Ireland.

It happens a second time in a Killarney supermarket where I am asking directions to the tea aisle.

On the third occasion as I am passing by, the owner invites me inside his Galway pub in the middle of the afternoon for a look and a pint. To be truthful, I am with four or five others, and we have a grand tour. We are treated like long lost cousins from America, which in fact, some of my group could be.

It has been quite some time since I have had conversations like that. There are sharing of opinions to be digested, rather than differences to be confronted.

I leave behind in the United States all the conservative/liberal hate talk for a month. It is a relief. And pure conversation for its own sake is a pleasant reminder of how lovely it can be.

Earlier in the week I visited Londonderry, or Derry, and walked the walled city and the outside streets to the peace bridge honoring the Good Friday Peace Agreement in 1998.

Here are the positive results of successful negotiations. Granted it isn't perfect yet. However, it's further from the years and years of bloody "Troubles" in the region.

A resident of Derry tells me, " First you must have conversation."

That statement resonates in my mind for the rest of that day, and I wonder if living side by side with other diverse people is a step to the advancement of global peace.

Once, I get a little confused and need assistance from someone to point me back in the right direction. I find out that the preferred way to ask for directions in Ireland is to turn the encounter into a social event, like when two strangers meet at a wedding reception.

Thus, I fall comfortably into conversation with an older gentleman donning his tam and walking stick. I have the usual explaining to do when he asks where I am from — "New York, but not the City of New York." We converse about his relatives living in Toronto. He can relate somewhat to my neck of the woods. I leave with his recommendation for two of his favorite pubs and a nearby botanical garden.

It never fails, but an independent bookstore is a perfect place to have a conversation with other avid bookies. Ireland has its share, and such stores are alive and well.

Hodges Figgis in Dublin offers a huge selection of Irish literature. When I pick up a small paperback book of contemporary stories by a local author, two sales clerks tell me how she is a personal writer friend. Of course, we three go on about our own writing, too. I am made to feel quite at home on a drizzly Sunday afternoon.

Someone remarks to me that what they love about the Irish is that they don't seem to be after your money. That is true of the Cork shop girls and the Dublin booksellers. The Irish want to know everything about you instead.

Yes, the Irish are talkers and writers with a quick wit. Theirs is an amazing literary past with four Pulitzer prizewinners in modern time. And storytellers. There are as numerous as small town pubs.

Perhaps that is why if you prefer to stay somewhat anonymous in your travels it is best to stick to larger cities and avoid small talk at all costs in rural places.

I stop for a cup of coffee in a tiny coastal town, and naturally, my camera is shooting pictures immediately. A woman about my age approaches and divulges with a twinkle in her eye that if I walk two blocks further north, I will find better flowers to photograph. We stroll together chatting, and yes, her gardens are magnificent.

A good rule of thumb in Ireland is to enter into a pub, stay for a drink and wait for something to happen. It will start with conversation and end with a fine evening of music by the peat fire. That is what the Irish have been doing for hundreds of years.

One Friday night I am in a three hundred year old thatch roof pub. It is pouring buckets outside, and I huddle near the blazing fireplace. Local folk are finishing dinner like anywhere else in the world, resting a bit at the end of a week's worth of work. A musical group generally doesn't start playing until people are warmed up with conversation. It is the center of everything Irish.

As the musician begins his repertoire of familiar tunes, a classic redheaded four-year old hops up on the stool behind him. She is dressed in her finery with her long hair pulled back with a blue ribbon. I assume that she is his daughter until he tells the audience later that she is a child that comes with her parents and listens spellbound for an hour at a time. She is hearing the tunes and absorbing the words oblivious that she is in a room full of people.

Ireland is an easy place to visit and feel right at home. I think that the people are very skilled at relating. There is fluidity to their language that makes it all sound so easy. It's a skill less developed with other nationalities, and for the Irish it is so instinctive; it doesn't even look like one.

I tap into the cultural warmth of Ireland and embrace it. Hopefully, I brought back a little bit of it, too. I'm looking forward to stopping on the street to have a chat with you.

Portrait of a Keyhole

A Stay in the Dromhall Hotel

"Alice: Would you tell me, please, which way I ought to go from here?
The Cheshire Cat: That depends a good deal on where you want to get to.
Alice: I don't much care where.
The Cheshire Cat: Then it doesn't much matter which way you go.
Alice: ...So long as I get somewhere.
The Cheshire Cat: Oh, you're sure to do that, if only you walk long enough."
   "Alice's Adventures in Wonderland" — Lewis Carroll

An old-fashioned shiny gold room key weighs down my left hand as if it is the tip on the daily Irish double race card that defeat is looming at the finish line.

It's a hotel key quite unlike the others that I use in Ireland. But then, Killarney is a city unto itself, a vibrant market town surrounded by loughs (lakes), and the Dromhall Hotel is a reflection of an elegant past lining up next to mammoth modern tourist chain hotels on the outskirts of town.

There is nothing welcoming about the Dromhall key either, like the convenient and quick key cards in most impersonal hotels. They are easy to slip in your purse, and unlike this one, which is to be turned over to the desk clerk when leaving the premises, the plastic cards keep you thinking no one knows you are away.

The five inch-long key dangles from a chrome loop and is engraved, "room 343." It is hilarious trying to open a hotel door with such a heavy key. It's not so amusing after working at it precisely for five minutes. I am sweating from frustration and tired from a long day of traveling. My trusty black waterproof pants and black long sleeved shirt are absorbing the moisture. They are slightly rumpled and ready to have a little refresher on the hanger from my hard work. I want in my room to clean up and take a quick nap.

I've never looked through a keyhole without finding someone was looking back. — Judy Garland

My eyes stare into the hole as if the way into the rabbit hole in *Alice and Wonderland*. I am trying to imagine the beautiful room on the other side all decked out waiting for me. There is a lovely queen bed with a pink floral patterned down comforter, lace edged white sheets and blue throw pillows as if artfully placed. At the far end of the room a sheer white floor length curtain makes light of any imperfection in the dark rose rug. The bathroom arrangement is small like European hotels with an ornate white enamel "step high to get over" tub that challenges the mobility of the most physically fit every morning. I am hoping my view is overlooking the hills and not the traffic circle on the main highway. There probably won't be Wi-Fi connection in the room, but the lobby is pleasant with its black spiral wrought iron staircase leading to our rooms and a pub with its dark wooden highlights off to the front side. It will give me a chance to socialize later. That is, if I gain entrance to my room, which is getting more and more doubtful.

The assistant manager greets our group in the lobby, and we receive a special lesson from him on how to open the door to our room. "Insert the key in and instantly go to the left while turning the door handle to the right. Push inward."

Simple enough.

Not so. Click. Click.

I am relocking the door and it is going nowhere fast like the words coming out of my mouth which are not so sweet. Up and down the hall others from my group make entry into their rooms. I am still standing here. Click. Click.

My hotel "next door neighbor" peeks out her door and sympathetically says that she will call the front desk for help.

I hear the shower running in one room. A window is opening in another. People are settling into their routines. I slump to the floor in defeat. This is my first — and will be my only snag — on the trip. It could be worse, and I drop my head in embarrassment as the cheerful clerk comes up the long hallway to assist. I remind myself that I can't be the only person, and later at dinner I am pleased to discover — I have to gloat here — that the two youngest grandchildren on the trip are simultaneously in the same predicament one floor below mine.

Apparently, the door is temperamental, and the clerk works at it jiggling the handle and lock. I practice a second time for comfort while the clerk is standing by.

The room is unlocked. The room is furnished every bit as I imagine from my telescopic view, and it will become my sanctuary.

I make the wise decision, and not a silly one. The foolish one first — I will not stay captive in my room out of fear of getting locked out and being made out to be the fool clothed in a simpleton's mind as played by Touchstone in *As You Like It*. To say that Touchstone is a clown is both a misnomer and an injustice. His knowledge, his wisdom, his wit and his faculty of observation, raise him far above the condition that such a definition would imply. And the wise one — I will take my chances and learn to relax with a tricky door-locking problem smarter as a result.

***

The key opens the door after a day out on the road doing the Ring of Kerry, a drive that traces the coastline of the Iveragh Peninsula and offers breathtaking views of sheep pastures. It isn't, "Oh no, one more sheep." It is more like, "What surprise will I come upon around the next bend in the road? Camera ready."

The key opens the door after an evening at a performance by the National Folk Theatre. Using the disciplines of traditional Irish music, dance, storytelling and mime, the group offers a cultural experience dramatizing the essence of Irish culture of a bygone era. I am mesmerized by the collection of actors celebrating the Blasket Islands from its earliest inhabitants to modern day reconnection.

The key opens the door a second day after a venture to the Dingle Peninsula and my first fresh fish and chips lunch with a condiment of vinegar in the coastal town of Dingle. The batter on the fish is fried crispy in texture when pulling it a part with my fork. It is as juicy and tender on the inside as if it is caught the moment I place my order.

***

The last turn of the latch closes my stay in Kilarney. The memories continue to linger and have not been shut out of my heart.

"And what is the use of a book," thought Alice, *"without pictures or conversation?"*
"Alice's Adventures in Wonderland" — Lewis Carroll

An Irish Sunday

There is a wisdom of the head, and a wisdom of the heart. — Charles Dickens

I should know better at my age and put old stereotypes to rest. First impressions aren't to be lasting ones.

The pub's lights are off, but it is open for business as usual, seven days a week. The massive black front door with its crooked latch is ajar enough to peer through illuminating the blinking Guinness signage on the picture window and casting a spell on the vertical worn down muted gray tiles running the length of the building. A distant sound of The Irish Rovers croon a welcome to the weary traveler bored from walking in and out of Dublin souvenir shops meant to lure the typical visitor's pocketbook.

The sleepy bartender looks up from his endless polishing of glasses, coming with the job description it seems, and points to the further corner where the tables are located.

It will do nicely.

I sit down to an Irish experience up close and intimate.

The faded red leather booth at the rear side of the bar is clinging to the smells from Saturday night's beer. It is a short distance around the paneled partition from the bar, and quiet enough in all respects to have a conversation and partake in a light lunch with my two travel friends: a woman close to my age and her eighteen-year-old granddaughter.

Early on in the week the three of us bond over the value of books in our lives, and today, we want to step back away from the swelling crowds and chat about our similar passion.

The dark wood-paneled walls leave little to the imagination and are covered with faded landscape pictures in cheap tin frames. The odd wall lighting fixture askew as if the place had seen a better balance, perhaps left over from last night's huge crowd, jolts my awareness that I am running upstream against the timely flow of pub visitors. Somewhere down the line of owners, a shelf of brown flasks of various sizes and shapes perches collected as a further dusty reminder of the age of this establishment.

The bartender comes to the table to greet us a second time — a proper couple sentences of greeting making us feel right at home— before assigning our feeding and care to the one waitress in the place. She appears out of the backroom and straightens her apron before pushing her brown hair back up into its ponytail. Both are lacking the usual energy of the Irish, and I remind myself that it is early in the schedule of a body's recuperation.

There is no menu other than the couple specials the freckle-faced gal rattles off to us like we are at the Sunday dinner table among family taking what's there graciously.

The Irish use the pub as a social club, and it is like sitting in the comfort of a friend's living room deep in philosophical talk, or lighter banter coming from familial roots. The drink is only secondary, and in my case, a respite from the long lines at Trinity College in Dublin viewing The Book of Kells for my few minutes portioned out before the vigilant guard taps my shoulder and moves me along to an even more intriguing sight.

The 19th century wall-lined bookshelves out of a Harry Potter script force me to sit down on one of the upholstered benches and imprint the scene in my head. I find no words. I wonder how anyone can pass through the long rectangular hall with its barrel ceiling without nodding reverently to real leather covered pieces of great literature — all my favorite Dickens' works systematically stacked in alphabetical order. Alas. Many, many people are shuffling through and crossing it off their personal bucket list.

***

Queen Elizabeth I in 1592 established Trinity College, officially known as the University of Dublin. Here is where you view the famous Book of Kells, an elaborate illuminated manuscript of the four Gospels. Created all by monks of St. Columba on the Isle of Iona around AD 800, the book contains lavishly illustrated manuscripts. This is one of the oldest surviving books in the world, and the quality of its artwork is the epitome of medieval craftsmanship and devotion.

***

Apparently my young book companion must feel as I do for she is intently scribbling in her journal her braids swaying back and forth as if they were the writing tools capturing the rhyme of her thoughts. She later tells me as we literally force ourselves to leave the hall that she wants to share this spell in time with her younger brother, also an avid reader. I ask her if she has placed the visual memory in her mind, and she hasn't thought to do that in a simple meditative process allowing the senses to take control emotionally. We return together to our unoccupied bench for I desire a second chance to observe the smells of worn leather and the various shades of tan in the volumes.

We locate her grandmother and all three of us decide it is time for lunch before museum visits in the afternoon. And I have discovered one more independent bookstore of Irish contemporary authors to browse through to feel the volumes as smooth as silk on the counter. That's where the raindrops will deposit me, and I will be oblivious to the outside drop in humidity.

After a brief walk along several streets we find the pub and get settled as I glance at my watch. It is ten minutes past noon. My Mormon companions laugh and remark that no one in Salt Lake City would believe where they are spending time on a Sunday morning. With a slight twinge of sinfulness floating to the surface of my mind, I let it go and am grateful that God is here everywhere all the time anyhow.

Our tour director seated at the bar with a glass of white wine and the *Dublin Times*, is taking a well-deserved break. The three of us have stumbled by accident upon his hideaway on a side street, and we give it no more thought.

The TV commentator is talking about a hurling match later in the afternoon between Cork and a neighboring town, and several other folks at the bar are hedging their bets in friendly rivalry. It is to be a championship match, and while resting in my hotel room, I will attempt to make sense out of a game I don't understand.

As for me, I butter my Irish soda bread and sip my corn chowder soup nodding to The Almighty my heavenly prayer for the Sabbath. All is well, very well with me in Ireland. My trip is coming to a close in a couple more days, and I am savoring each and every minute slowing the adventure down as best as I can.

Worshipping an intense love of books at Trinity College with Charles Dickens's spirit over my shoulder requires an Irish pub on a late Sunday morn feasting with God in real time.

Life is made of ever so many partings welded together.
— Charles Dickens

My Fondest Memories

Barry's Irish Tea. The Dingle Peninsula. Pub crawls. Wedding reception. Bookstores. Dampness. Fish and chips. Book of Kelles. Bogs. Weaving. W.B.Yeats. Castles. Stone fences. Hillsides. Walking sticks. Crystal bowls. Thatched roofs. Laughter. Rain. Living history. Impromptu conversations. Euros. Sincerity. Rose petals. Potato soups. Cemeteries. Mist. Friendships. Markets. Dublin cheeses. Hotel lobbies. Energetic music. Peace Bridge. American flags. Titanic Museum. Pound sterling. Red hair. Irish linens. Sheep dogs. Salmon. Cliffs of Moher. Black wrought iron fences. Irish folks and their ways are the real deal no question about it.

Acknowledgements

I am grateful to the Irish people and their welcoming attitude. I was not expecting it, but I should have known better.

When Irish eyes are smiling sure 'tis like a morn in spring.
In the lilt of Irish laughter, you can hear the angels sing.

As much as a writer resists someone else fussing with his work, it is a necessary evil. Thanks to the conversations and content guidance, DJ Smith.

I thank Kate Stiffler, an excellent proofreader. Her expertise makes the book complete. Our friendship flourishes, too.

I credit the cover and graphic design to my husband, Larry. He lived through the whole process from beginning to end.

Check the author's website, www.kathomaswriter.com for a collection of pictures from the trip.

Made in the USA
Charleston, SC
30 March 2014